THE 15 REVOLUTION

GO AHEAD INCONVENIENCE ME

Abundant Life Publishing

Wapping Road, Bradford, West Yorkshire, BD3 0EQ

The personal stories in this book were first submitted to the *15 Revolution* website: **www.15revolution.com**. The contributors have subsequently agreed to the use of these edited versions in this publication. Their stories remain accurate but names have been changed as for personal privacy.

First Published in 2009

British Library Cataloguing in Publication Data:

A catalogue record for this book is available from the British Library.

ISBN: 13 978-0-9555804-4-4

15 Revolution

CONTENTS

Introduction

THE 15 REVOLUTION

The *15 Revolution* is as simple - and as difficult - as being willing to give 15 minutes a day to be inconvenienced in order to help someone. It is being willing to give 15 minutes a day to be interrupted, distracted, diverted or delayed. 15 minutes to add value to someone else's world.

The *15 Revolution* is not an outreach event or missions programme, which as good as they are, by definition can only mobilise a relatively small number of people. Many such programmes are focussed into an overseas or distant regional context and, vital as they are, can leave our own backyards unreached. In contrast, the *15 Revolution* mobilises everyone to do something right where they are and to do it now. It has nothing to do with training, calling, gifting or personality; it's simply changing your world 15 minutes at a time.

It sounds simple, I know, but what makes it difficult is how 'hard wired' we are against being inconvenienced, interrupted or delayed. Our brains are increasingly programmed for speed as modern civilisation revs itself into an ever-shorter attention span. To slow down is anti-cultural and anti-social. But many are discovering that to get fast acting relief from stress, you have to try slowing down. *'Be still and know that I am God'*

(Psalm 46:10) isn't just a nice verse for a fridge magnet, it's a pointer towards how we can get to know more about God and his nature. In our driven, fast paced western lifestyles, we rarely even notice anything or anyone not essential to our daily routines. We are becoming a less relational world, less engaging of each other and less trusting of strangers.

Maybe like me you watched CNN with horror as it showed the CCTV footage of a woman dying in a hospital emergency waiting room, whilst three people sat watching it happen without lifting a finger to help. A week later, also on CNN, I watched traffic camera footage of a man who had been hit by a car as he tried to cross a street in New York. As he staggered to stand up, cars swerved around him and pedestrians just watched, again without lifting a finger to help him. I understand the fear of involving in another person's problems, lawsuits and possible personal injuries all loom large in a world where the threat of litigation has de-humanised us towards each other. But I do believe that our need for speed has isolated us and made us blind to the needs of our fellow human beings.

The *15 Revolution* sets out to reverse this trend, to make us more aware of the people in our immediate space and to provoke us to be the bringers of God's life to the hurting world on our doorstep. It is that simple and it is that difficult! If you are willing to consciously give at least 15 minutes a day to be inconvenienced in order to help someone, read on and join the revolution.

Chapter 1

GO AHEAD, INCONVENIENCE ME!

How willing are you to be inconvenienced for others? This question is at the core of the *15 Revolution*. In fact the first step you have to take when you join this revolution is one of being willing to be inconvenienced. You have to put on an imaginary sign which says 'Go ahead, inconvenience me!' I say 'imaginary' because it starts in your mind. You have to change the way you think about people and approach situations. You have to begin actually looking for opportunities to be inconvenienced!

The *15 Revolution* stories included in this book illustrate just how hard people have had to work to overcome the inconvenience factor. It takes real resolve to deal with the 'I can't be bothered', 'I don't have time', and the 'this will take too long' moment; the moments when the inconvenience of it all bites harder than anything else, and beckons us to turn back, withdraw, move on, or leave it for another time. Most of us never survive those moments because inconvenience is always real and totally reasonable.

Personally, I hate to be inconvenienced and, like the rest of us, enjoy all the things our western world provides to minimise inconvenience. So, having spent our lives avoiding inconvenience and then suddenly deciding to choose it by deliberately reaching out to someone, creates a sense of seeming contradiction. We must deal with this ruthlessly; every revolution has its enemies and for this one, it is inconvenience.

Jesus taught us how to beat this enemy through some of his best known parables. For example, the parable of the Wedding Banquet in Luke chapter 14. In this story each of the invited guests sent a last minute, 'sorry I can't make it' reply. They no doubt made a range of excuses along the lines of being too busy, the event not being important enough, or having other pressing engagements.

Imagine the huge inconvenience this caused to the banquet host, who in the parable is representative of God. Everything was ready; no expense had been spared, the food was cooked, the room hired and all he needed was the guests. But they declined. How inconvenient! Instead of caving into their apathy, the host tells his servants to go and find others who were not on the original guest list but who may be glad of the opportunity. He pressed beyond the huge initial inconvenience, further inconvenienced his staff and just kept reaching more people until the banquet was filled. You see, God is always willing to be inconvenienced to reach someone and so must we.

Have you any idea how inconvenient it was to reach you? I wonder how often we have cancelled the party because we felt others were being inconvenienced by our efforts? Or more importantly, how often we have withdrawn or failed to involve because of our own feelings of being inconvenienced. It all becomes just too much trouble. When this feeling creeps over us, we must show the same resolve as the master in this story. We must put up our imaginary sign, get in amongst people and effectively say, 'Go ahead, inconvenience me!'

This attitude reminds me of another of Jesus' parables, the one about the Persistent Widow in Luke chapter 18. She was a pest! She unstintingly pestered and inconvenienced her local judge to grant her justice against her adversary. The judge neither feared God nor cared about people, yet he eventually gave in and helped her simply because she was so persistent. Persistence always overcomes apathy and inconvenience.

Life teaches us that all too often the best things in life - its greatest breakthroughs, miracles and memories - seem to be deliberately placed just beyond our convenient reach. The greatest things in life are protected by just enough problems, set backs and inconveniences. This ensures that only those who really want to make a difference will be granted entry to where amazing things can happen. That is why I chose 'Go ahead, inconvenience me!' as the tag line for the *15 Revolution*.

If we invite inconvenience, it can no longer intimidate us. Jesus said, *'if they make you walk a mile, offer to walk two. If they demand your shirt, give them your coat too' (Matthew 5:41 - Message).*

In other words, make it your idea, make friends with inconvenience. I don't mean be a doormat for people's inefficiency or gratuitous inconvenience - God knows I would never be the one to encourage that! But we are going to have to step outside of our routines, plans and agendas if we want to join the *15 Revolution* and embrace inconvenience as our friend.

My gay hairdresser

by Paul Scanlon

Recently on my day off I had my hair cut by a guy who doesn't normally do it. My usual hairdresser James was away so they offered me this other guy called Richard. After telling him how I liked it cutting, I relaxed and retreated into my newspaper. I didn't exactly have a 'please do disturb' sign on my life.

It's convenient keeping the same people in your life. After three years my regular hairdresser knows me. He knows a bit about my family, what I do etc, and I know the same about him. All that familiar ground makes it easy to just kind of catch up when he cuts my hair.

Richard, the new guy, asked me what seems to be the standard hairdresser question, 'What do you do?' This immediately made me feel uncomfortable and inconvenienced. You must understand that in England the 'C' word 'church' is like a dirty word. Statistics show that 98% of our population don't attend church and most of them seem 'anti' rather than 'pro' church.

To say I work at a church is usually an instant conversation killer, because it's a word that's totally irrelevant to most people. But I remembered my *15 Revolution* commitment and told him I was the pastor of a church in the locality. He replied, 'Well that's interesting. I'm a Catholic and recently my parents invited me to their Catholic church'. He continued, 'I told them I couldn't go because, as they knew, the Pope has just made a statement against homosexuality and I am gay and my parents friends at church know I'm gay, so I didn't want to be an inconvenience'.

I realised whatever I said next was going to be important. He paused, then asked me, 'Do you welcome gay people at your church?' I paused, and almost without thinking the answer came from my spirit, then my brain caught up and realised that my answer was a flash of wisdom to help my own life. I said, 'No we don't welcome gay people, we just welcome people' (and by the way, a welcome doesn't mean that you endorse a person's lifestyle. Jesus welcomed all). He said 'What do you mean?' I said, 'Well, we don't welcome categories of people, we don't have sections for homosexuals, straight etc, we just welcome everyone'. My point being that when Jesus died on the cross, he didn't spend the first hour for all the normal sinners, and then do the next twenty minutes for homosexuals, then the next ten minutes for prostitutes, then ten minutes for murderers and so on. He died once for all people! And yet we, the church, seem to categorise people according to lifestyles. To cut a long story short, I invited Richard to church, and the following Sunday evening he came. He was there for two reasons, firstly because I decided to be inconvenienced and secondly, I decided not to judge him. I learned a huge lesson that day, because I had been inviting James to church for three years, but he never came. The new guy was open to do something immediately that James hadn't been open to in three years. Often the least responsive people are the most time consuming, and the most responsive are the ones we ignore because it's too inconvenient to include them.

Chapter 2

WHO IS MY NEIGHBOUR?

Jesus was once asked, 'Who is my neighbour?' He answered by telling the famous story of the Good Samaritan *(Luke 10)*. A man was beaten up, robbed and left to die by the roadside. Along came a priest, who saw the man but passed by on the other side of the road, as did the next guy who was another churchgoer. The third person to come across the dying man was a Samaritan. The Samaritans were avowed enemies of the Jews to whom Jesus was telling this story. The Samaritan saw the injured man, felt pity, crossed the street and helped him by bandaging his wounds. He then took him to a hotel where he paid for the man to stay until he was well enough to leave. This foreigner had been the true neighbour to the injured man.

So, at the core of Jesus' definition of 'my neighbour' is the thought that my neighbour is anyone who is willing to be inconvenienced to help me. The *15 Revolution* is a commitment to once again become the world's true neighbour by living with a 'please do disturb' sign on our lives and with a 'Go ahead, inconvenience me!' badge always on display.

This is not evangelism

The *15 Revolution* is not about evangelism as most Christians define that term today. Sadly, we have often evangelised without loving people. We have all too frequently seen unsaved people as evangelistic challenges to be conquered rather than people to be loved, enjoyed and served.

It has been my observation that too many church leaders, me included, have taught evangelism so poorly that it became all about church growth and not about people. The emphasis was on getting converts, making disciples and raising up leaders - all of which are good, but it became all about the numbers. The truth is that all these things are ultimately achieved by loving people from the very first point of contact onwards.

As I reflect on some of the evangelistic approaches that have been popular at different times during the last 30 years, it seems to me the approach has often got in the way of the person being reached. We have taught power evangelism, prophetic evangelism and divine appointment evangelism, to name but three, all of which often bred a very intense, super spiritual form of Christianity. We were encouraged to look for the 'special' ones who are open to God, rather than just loving all amongst whom the 'special' ones live. I'm not closed to the idea of God leading us to individuals who may be more open, but it's not wise to teach this as a general approach because upon hearing it, most people rule themselves out as not being gifted or wired that way. Or worse still, they go out and try too hard to have a divine appointment, usually resulting in what looks like an evangelistic assault on an unsuspecting bystander rather than anything divine.

Christians and non-Christians both have something in common, we both dislike evangelism. Christians dislike it because we feel awkward and non-Christians dislike it because we are awkward. It only takes one unpleasant evangelistic experience to put both Christians and non-Christians off it for life.

The *15 Revolution* is not about evangelism, it's a revolution of love, interest and compassion for people. It is learning to live, as it were, with your head on 'swivel' as you begin to notice the people who were always there, but you couldn't see because you were looking for converts rather than a connection with people.

Evangelism without compassion is a loveless duty and compassion is not fuelled by duty, but God's amazing grace.

Compassion quota

The *15 Revolution* is all about increasing our personal compassion quota. Helping others in any sustained way has to be compassion driven. Duty, obligation and guilt etc can all motivate us, but they lack long-term sustainability. Compassion keeps going in the face of a poor response. Its reward is not a favourable reaction but simply the fulfilment that comes from helping others. Being a Christian doesn't make you compassionate or inclusive of others. If that were true then every church would be bursting at the seams. Being a Christian simply places us in the privileged category of those to whom God has been compassionate. That reality should be all the motivation we ever need to help someone else.

Compassion is fuelled by empathy, a sense of walking in another person's shoes. That empathy-fuelled compassion then thinks about how to make those shoes easier to walk in. Compassion is a sign, a clue to why we are here. What we feel empathy for is probably something we are gifted to fix, improve and make a difference to. Yet we have developed a culture of people trying to find what they're good at by pursuing titles, positions and roles, but they have no real passion for the work that comes with it. Increased compassion makes us better people. Compassion notices things, spots opportunities to help and looks for ways to ease suffering. I don't want a highly gifted church that doesn't really care about our city. As Paul said, *'If we speak in the tongues of angels but have not love, what's the point?' (1 Corinthians 13:1 - Message)*

The *15 Revolution* is fuelled by compassion. Compassion increases by helping others and forgetting about ourselves. The resulting condition is called Christianity.

The *15 Revolution* will not work if we are seeing it as a means to a greater end or as evangelism. People have asked me 'but don't we have a responsibility to tell people about Jesus?'

My reply has been that the *15 Revolution* is not so much about growing our churches as it is about growing ourselves first. It's not about increasing our evangelism quota but our compassion quota. And I confidently say this without worrying about our church growth because a compassionate church will always grow, but an evangelistic church without compassion won't.

A neighbour to my neighbour

Angela's Story

I'd just got back home after a long haul flight, landing at Gatwick airport at 6.40am. By the time I got home it was mid afternoon, so I'm sure you can appreciate that I was feeling just a little tired at this point, having been awake for 24 hours straight.

Whilst I was away, my neighbour had given birth to her second child, a little girl. I remembered how she struggled after having her first child back in 2006, so I went to say hello before I had even set foot in my own house. As soon as she opened the door, I could tell by the look on her face that she was in need of a shoulder to cry on. Her face crumpled, and tears began to roll down her face. As you can imagine, I was hoping to have a quick coo over the baby, hug my neighbour in a congratulatory manner, and then head home to scrub off the aeroplane grime. I felt as if I needed to prop my eyelids open with a matchstick, but I stepped into my neighbour's house as I could see she needed me at that point. My neighbour was having real problems feeding her baby. I've got two children, one of whom I fed until she was 16 months old, so I understood how she was feeling about it all. We talked through everything she could do to make things easier. I changed baby's nappy, cuddled the baby to give my neighbour a break (and indulge myself, because there's nothing so lovely as that new baby smell!) I must have been there almost half an hour before I felt I could leave her. She was a lot calmer after having talked it through with me and was feeling more positive about how she was doing with her new baby. She had been beating herself up about being a bad mother, which was not even vaguely true, but her post natal hormones had kicked in nicely, leaving her feeling horrendous.

I am so glad I pushed myself to spend that time with her. It was only half an hour, but it was when I myself was completely exhausted. It helped her so much. She has since thanked me for going out of my way that day. My *15 Revolution* (or 30 minute as it ended up being) left me feeling good, even though I was tired, smelly and ready to soak in the bath!

Chapter 3

REVOLUTIONARIES NOT REBELS

In the closing moments of Jesus' life the crowd were given the option of either freeing Jesus, an innocent man, or freeing Barabbas, a known rebel leader and murderer *(Matthew 27:17)*. It beggars belief that they shouted 'let Barabbas go free and crucify Jesus'. But the truth is that the world will always choose a rebel over a revolutionary.

Rebels are against something - **Revolutionaries** are for something.
Rebels curse the darkness - **Revolutionaries** shine the light.
Rebels march against - **Revolutionaries** walk amongst.
Rebels recruit - **Revolutionaries** reproduce.
Rebels resist - **Revolutionaries** replace.

Rebels want to overthrow someone or something but have no better ideas with which to replace it, whereas a revolutionary has a new idea, an alternative to what exists and isn't working anymore. Nelson Mandela, Martin Luther King and Gandhi were all revolutionaries. Jesus was the greatest revolutionary of all time. He came with the biggest replacement idea ever and it was called the Kingdom of God.

The barking dog

I hate the fact that much of the church has become famous for its intolerance of the world. We are known for what we are against, whether it's abortion, homosexuality, smoking, alcohol or Harry Potter. You name it, the church is against it. Now I'm not particularly advocating any of the above, my point here is that we have become the angry dog that barks at every passer by. Eventually the dog just becomes an irritant in the neighbourhood. The neighbours avoid the dog, but can never forget it because like all barking dogs, much of the time it just barks for no reason.

I don't want to 'bark' at my city or the people in it. I want to appreciate it, love it and learn to live amongst the people of my city as a revolutionary for positive change.

The *15 Revolution* is a no-brainer in terms of loving our towns and cities. I promise you, it is revolutionary to stop what you are doing or divert from where you were going and notice someone who you could help.

Jesus was not known for what he was against. He was not known as the 'Pharisee hater' or the 'Tax Collector's worst nightmare'! Instead he was famous for the good he did for people. He was called the healer, the one who spoke with authority and wisdom, the great teacher. But most notably, he was called the 'friend of sinners'. What a reputation to have! And we, Christ's Body in the world today, should have the same reputation.

The church is not a resistance movement; it is a replacement movement. God so loved the world that he didn't send us an ultimatum but an alternative.

The rearranged day

Brian's Story

My wife and I run a home computer support company. Early in 2007 we had a call from Peter, a man in his eighties who wanted help with word processing and transferring a lifetime's slides onto his computer. Once every two weeks for nearly a year I visited and we had our lesson.

On Christmas Eve 2007 we called to take Peter and Muriel, his wife, a small gift and a card. When we arrived they were both in tears, his doctor had told him that morning that he had liver cancer and only had a few months to live. Peter died in the spring of 2008. We called a few times through the year to see Muriel but not as often as we should.

On Tuesday I had a couple of hours' gap between two appointments so I thought I would do the shopping. As I drove to the supermarket I felt God say to me 'Go and see Muriel'. But I reasoned that if I went to see her I wouldn't have time to do the shopping, so I'd make time to see her tomorrow. 'What about your pledge to be inconvenienced?' God countered. I turned the car around and drove to her house. She was surprised but pleased to see me. As we chatted I said 'It must be nearly a year since Peter died'. She replied 'It is exactly a year today, I have just come back from taking flowers to his grave and I need someone to talk to'. Talk about timing!

At one point she asked if I thought God loved her. I told her he must do as he rearranged my entire day and prompted me to be there to tell her just that.

Chapter 4

JUST STOP!

At the heart of this *15 Revolution* is a renewed commitment to slow down and stop for someone.

Stopping becomes increasingly difficult the busier we get. The more people that travel with us and rely on us, the more difficult it is to stop. When Jesus stopped, the whole crowd had to stop. Everyone was inconvenienced, not just Jesus. Often it's the inconvenience to those around us that prevents us stopping to help someone.

I honestly believe that more people have been missed through our unwillingness to be inconvenienced than almost anything else - the last minute hesitation, that concern about how long it will take, the fear of getting involved and where it might end up taking us, the concern about being late for our appointment, missing our bus or letting someone down. In the story of the Good Samaritan, he didn't set out that day to spend hours helping an injured stranger; no doubt he was on a schedule too but was willing to just stop, take notice and be inconvenienced.

Please don't think that the *15 Revolution* is about giving huge amounts of time. Many of the stories I receive are from people taking a few seconds or minutes to add value to someone else. But those few minutes required them first to just stop. That's what Jesus did. He just stopped one day as he was travelling with the large crowd around him:

'As Jesus and his disciples, together with a large crowd, were leaving the city, a blind man, Bartimaeus (that is, the Son of Timaeus), was sitting by the roadside begging. When he heard that it was Jesus of Nazareth, he began to shout, "Jesus, Son of David, have mercy on me!" Many rebuked him and told him to be quiet, but he shouted all the more, "Son of David, have mercy on me!"

Jesus stopped *and said, "Call him." So they called to the blind man, "Cheer up! On your feet! He's calling you." Throwing his cloak aside, he jumped to his feet and came to Jesus. "What do you want me to do for you?" Jesus asked him. The blind man said, "Rabbi, I want to see."*

"Go," said Jesus, "your faith has healed you." Immediately he received his sight and followed Jesus along the road.' (Mark 10:46-52)

Jesus stopped even though there was a crowd urging him forward, even though he had a place to get to by nightfall and even though there were opposing voices in the crowd. Jesus just stopped for one person. Will you? It may take you 15 seconds, 15 minutes or 15 hours. But isn't one changed life worth it?

Compliments count

Just stopping is not only about pausing for a dramatic miracle, it can be as ordinary as paying someone a compliment. Adding value to a person's day, encouraging them or pausing to help, can actually be just as miraculous for the person concerned. So don't underestimate the power of your pause or the significance of your stopping to the person concerned.

How long does it take to compliment someone? A compliment can be such an easy and generous way to engage with people. I recently complimented a waiter on his shoes. He was so appreciative that we ended up in a long conversation about our lives, and to cut a long story short he came to hear me speak at the church I was visiting on the Sunday. A compliment costs you nothing, needs no training, preparation or skill, yet can build great self-esteem in the recipient. A compliment is an act of kindness and generosity.

One day I was in Starbucks in a town in the 'Bible belt' of America with a few Pastor friends. The girl serving me had a spiky Mohawk hairstyle as well as some body piercing, tattoos and black make-up. She was a bit of a Goth I think. I said 'Hey I really like your hair, how long does it take to do that?' She seemed pleasantly surprised and instantly brightened up and began explaining her hair routine. I told her one of my sons-in-law often has a Mohawk and sometimes he bleaches the tips. I wondered if she had ever thought of trying that. She said she hadn't but thought it was a great idea and would try it. She then asked me what I did. When I told her I was a Pastor, she said 'We get lots of church people in here, but you're the first to ever compliment me on the way I look'. Later, my Pastor friends said that they had felt challenged by the way I spoke to her, because their first thoughts were more in the direction of 'what a shame that she had done that to herself'. I really appreciated their honesty, because a few years ago that would have been my reaction.

In recent years I have become less judgmental, less stereotyping of people and far less concerned about a person's outward appearance. If Jesus conceals himself amongst the poor, naked and hungry, then I guess he could easily be the Goth in Starbucks.

You may feel inadequate in evangelism but you can compliment someone, notice someone's shoes, clothes, jewellery, or even their tattoo or Mohawk. This *15 Revolution* is a revolution of connecting with people, not trying to convert people. And the art of connecting with people has by and large been lost to a 'conversion only' minded church.

Slow down

If you can't stop, then start by slowing down. Start by noticing people, by being aware of others. Lift your head up a little, take the blinkers off, enjoy the journey, uncouple from the clock for just a moment. Some of the greatest miracles will never happen unless someone slows down. Some of the greatest connections will never happen unless someone slows down. Some of the greatest songs ever written and ideas ever thought up will never happen unless someone slows down.

Remember, someone once slowed down and stopped for you and me. The *15 Revolution* is about slowing down and stopping for just 15 minutes a day. Can you do that? Just remember that doing it once or twice isn't a revolution, it's not a revolution until it becomes a new behavior. But the good thing is you need no training, preparation or skill to start doing this. So, keep your eyes open and get ready to slow down and just stop for someone today.

The old lady who slowed me down

By Paul Scanlon

I was running to catch my connecting flight from Chicago to London. My inbound flight was delayed giving me only minutes to catch my London flight. I was allowed to the front of the security line, only to get stuck behind an old lady who was slowly placing her belongings on the conveyer belt. At that moment a security staff person stepped in front of us and said 'your London flight has closed its doors, you are too late, you must step out of the line and go back to check-in and they will re-assign you for tomorrow evening's flight'.

At that news the old lady just broke down in tears and became very distraught saying that she was travelling alone for the first time as a 76 year old recent widow. She had no money to stay overnight and didn't understand what re-assigned meant. The security staff member just barked at her, 'Mam, you need to step out of the line, you are holding everyone up.' I honestly thought she was going to have a heart attack. Here was my *15 Revolution* opportunity. I grabbed her hand and said, 'you stick with me, we are going to get on that flight'. She squeezed my hand and said to me, 'Are you an angel?' I said 'No, but I am going to help you'.

I began helping her through security, helping her take her shoes off, handbag, carry-on bag, coat and walking stick. It was at this point I realised that not only could I be in trouble with security but also that this inconvenience of stopping to help this old lady could stop me catching the flight too. We got through security and because the gate was a long way off, I flagged down an airport passenger golf cart. I explained our dilemma to the driver and while explaining that he probably shouldn't really allow us on board, I was already loading my new found friend on the back, knowing that no self respecting golf cart driver would throw an old lady off!

We arrived at the gate. The plane doors were still open and I explained to the cabin crew what had happened. They took the lady still crying and helped her on board. I sat down in my seat in Business Class, relieved that we got the flight. Moments later I looked across to my right and there, sat with her feet up drinking champagne, was my old lady friend. She smiled at me and said 'Hello again, they felt so sorry for me that they upgraded me from economy, did they upgrade you too?' I replied 'No, I paid for my seat and it wasn't cheap so that's a big thing they have done for you.' She said 'Oh, I kept telling everyone that God sent me an angel today, I wouldn't be here without your help.' I smiled and said 'You're welcome' then reclined my seat to rest.

She obviously had other plans. She came and sat next to me and talked my ears off for the next six hours! As I drove home from the airport I smiled to myself and said to God, 'I can take a month off now because there's a lot of 15 minutes in 6 hours'! My point is that to help her, I risked being held up. To help her, I had to slow down. Interestingly she told everyone that an angel had helped her. She didn't say a demon, but an angel. People always associate goodness with

God because all goodness, whoever it comes through, is ultimately from God and I believe that all people fundamentally believe that. We the Church are here to make goodness fashionable, current, relevant, mainstream and commonplace. And we can do it 15 minutes at a time.

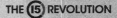

Chapter 5

GOODNESS LEADS TO CHANGE

The Bible says that the goodness of God leads people to repentance *(Romans 2:4 KJV)*. Modern translations replace goodness with kindness and the *15 Revolution* is all about doing good and being kind. However, the problem with this scripture is that we have interpreted thc word repentance as only meaning full conversion to Christ. So we expect too much to come from our acts of kindness and they all too often become loaded with our selfish evangelistic agenda.

Repentance doesn't mean conversion but simply change. Repentance means to change direction, change ones mind. With that understanding we can restate that scripture as really saying 'the goodness of God leads people to change their mind'. Goodness changes people, goodness can be overwhelming, barrier-breaking and disarming. Goodness produces gratitude in people and grateful people become more inclined to help others.

The *15 Revolution* is a revolution of acts of goodness and kindness, often on the smallest of scales but accumulating to have the largest of impacts.

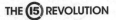

Pass it on

It seems that one of the things which most angers God is when people who have received goodness, kindness or forgiveness do not pass it on. Jesus told a story that makes this point with great effect.

The context was a conversation between Jesus and Simon Peter, one of his closest friends. Peter had no doubt been quite a character and, in Jesus, had found a way to receive God's forgiveness for his wrongs as well as being able to forgive himself. He had been forgiven much. His dilemma now was, just how forgiving should he be towards all the annoying people in his world who kept letting him down and then asking for his forgiveness?

'Then Peter came to Jesus and asked, "Lord, how many times shall I forgive my brother when he sins against me? Up to seven times?" Jesus answered, "I tell you, not seven times, but seventy-seven times."' (Matthew 18:21-22)

You can imagine Peter reeling at the thought of having to forgive people so many times. Maybe he wondered whether he should keep a list so that he would know when he hit the magic 77th time and could stop forgiving them! And surely this was a totally unreasonable amount anyway. Who ever deserved to be forgiven so many times? But as he reeled back, Jesus continued with the story of the Unmerciful Servant to illustrate the point:

'Therefore, the kingdom of heaven is like a king who wanted to settle accounts with his servants. As he began the settlement, a man who owed him ten thousand talents was brought to him. Since he was not able to pay, the master ordered that he and his wife and his children and all that he had be sold to repay the debt. The servant fell on his knees before him. "Be patient with me," he begged, "and I will pay back everything." The servant's master took pity on him, cancelled the debt and let him go.

But when that servant went out, he found one of his fellow servants who owed him a hundred denarii. He grabbed him and began to choke him. "Pay back what you owe me!" he demanded. His fellow servant fell to his knees and begged him, "Be patient with me, and I will pay you back." But he refused. Instead, he went off and had the man thrown into prison until he could pay the debt.

When the other servants saw what had happened, they were greatly distressed and went and told their master everything that had happened. Then the master called the servant in. "You wicked servant," he said, "I cancelled all that debt of yours because you begged me to. Shouldn't you have had mercy on your fellow servant just as I had on you?" In anger his master turned him over to the jailers to be tortured, until he should pay back all he owed.
This is how my heavenly Father will treat each of you unless you forgive your brother from your heart.' (Matthew 18:23–35)

This sobering story makes the point with clarity. We must pass it on! The goodness we have received from God and other people, we must pass on to others in equal measures of generosity and grace.

The incident where Jesus cursed the fig tree for not having any figs was not about him having a bad day and taking it out on the tree! It was an insight into God's expectations for all living, growing things. This tree was a living violation of its creation mandate. It was receiving without passing on. We too share the same creational mandate, and as believers a conversion mandate, to pass on the life we have received to others.

The most basic biblical qualification for helping others is not theology, experience, training or expertise. The most basic qualification for helping others is that you have been helped yourself. If you have been helped, then you are over-qualified to help others. Yet so many of us who have had so much help still live with a consumer mentality as if it's all about us and our needs. This must change if we are to truly play our part in the *15 Revolution.*

Mr Grumpy

Clare's Story

I work for a greeting card company and have to go in and out of a busy warehouse in a supermarket to collect stock, but am always being shouted at by the senior man - known to all as Mr Grumpy! My efforts to be polite are met with 'shut up talking, get your head down and start working!' Or he simply points at the exit and shouts 'GET OUT!'

Mr Grumpy is not my favourite man as you can imagine, so when I told my husband all about him, I expected plenty of sympathy, but instead I gained a new understanding. My husband explained that because warehouses can be dangerous places, with fork lift trucks driven at full speed and huge containers being constantly loaded and unloaded, people like Mr Grumpy are actually saving lives when they shout! A well run warehouse can make or break a company, and be the key to success when they deal with goods safely and efficiently. This new perspective helped me feel respect for this man instead of fear, and one day I decided I would inconvenience myself and risk having my head bitten off to speak to him. I said 'Can I say something to you please?' He had his back to me and didn't turn round, but I could see him stiffen up as though he was getting ready to shout at me to go away. My natural instinct was to forget it, but I pressed through that feeling and continued 'I just wanted to say I think you are doing a great job in this warehouse, and my husband told me that a warehouse is actually the key to success in a supermarket so thank you for everything you do.' I felt a bit stupid but there it was.

I didn't expect to get a reply and didn't get one and just went about my business. But since then Mr Grumpy has changed beyond all recognition! Instead of shouting, he now politely informs me that my deliveries have arrived. He looks after my stock, stacking them neatly near his desk. And I nearly fell over backwards one day when he actually smiled at me! It was such an unexpected surprise! I now have a huge respect for this man and he shows me respect in return, but I would never have guessed that this would be the outcome of taking just 15 seconds (not even 15 minutes) to honour him with a little compliment, recognition and appreciation.

How many other Mr Grumpys in our world are starving for just that?

Chapter 6

THOSE WHO HAPPENED TO BE THERE

The *15 Revolution* is all about noticing, including, helping and adding value to people in your world. To try and re-enforce that it's not about looking for divine appointments or evangelistic encounters, I want us to look at the experience of the Apostle Paul in Athens. I have included the whole passage so you understand the full context before we explore it together in the next three chapters:

'While Paul was waiting for them in Athens, he was greatly distressed to see that the city was full of idols. So he reasoned in the synagogue with the Jews and the God-fearing Greeks, as well as in the marketplace day by day ***with those who happened to be there.*** *A group of Epicurean and Stoic philosophers began to dispute with him. Some of them asked, "What is this babbler trying to say?" Others remarked, "He seems to be advocating foreign gods." They said this because Paul was preaching the good news about Jesus and the resurrection.*

Then they took him and brought him to a meeting of the Areopagus, where they said to him, "May we know what this new teaching is that you are presenting? You are bringing some strange ideas to our ears, and we want to know what they mean." (All the Athenians and the foreigners who lived there spent their time doing nothing but talking about and listening to the latest ideas.) Paul then stood up in the meeting of the Areopagus and said: "Men of Athens! I see that in every way you are very religious. For as I walked around and looked carefully at your objects of worship, I even found an altar with this inscription: TO AN UNKNOWN GOD. Now what you worship as something unknown I am going to proclaim to you.

The God who made the world and everything in it is the Lord of heaven and earth and does not live in temples built by hands. And he is not served by human hands, as if he needed anything, because he himself gives all men life and breath and everything else. From one man he made every nation of men, that they should inhabit the whole earth; and he determined the times set for them and the exact places where they should live. God did this so that men would seek him and perhaps reach out for him and find him, though he is not far from each one of us. 'For in him we live and move and have our being.' As some of your own poets have said, 'We are his offspring.'

Therefore since we are God's offspring, we should not think that the divine being is like gold or silver or stone – an image made by man's design and skill. In the past God overlooked such ignorance, but now he commands all people everywhere to repent. For he has set a day when he will judge the world with justice by the man he has appointed. He has given proof of this to all men by raising him from the dead." When they heard about the resurrection of the dead, some of them sneered, but others said, "We want to hear you again on this subject." At that, Paul left the Council. A few men became followers of Paul and believed. Among them was Dionysius, a member of the Areopagus, also a woman named Damaris, and a number of others.' (Acts 17:16–34)

This story just shouts *15 Revolution* to me! Let me explain. Paul is killing time in Athens whilst waiting for some of his team to join him. While looking around he becomes very distressed about the obvious spiritual confusion in the city. It is full of idols and just to be sure none has been overlooked there was even one to an 'Unknown God'.

Please note here that Paul's distress was an expression of his compassion. Before Paul moved on the outside he was moved on the inside. These tiny comments and observations that Dr. Luke makes as he writes the book of Acts are absolute gems of insight into the 'why' not just the 'what' of the historical account. Many of us live in cities far worse than Athens ever was and yet we have never felt distressed about it. I believe this says something about our compassion, our felt sense of distress, as we pass through our cities unmoved by the human tragedy all around us. To evangelise without first being distressed is to promote activity over empathy. Paul was like Jesus, who was first moved with compassion and then began to help people *(Mark 6:34)*.

Next, note where Paul went. On feeling distressed he went first to the place where God's people gathered - to the church - and then to the marketplace. In both he taught and reasoned, first with those most likely to understand his spiritual perspective, which is what we may well have done. But having made little progress he does the same in the market place, publicly expressing his concern for the spiritual well-being of the Athenians.

Luke tells us that Paul spoke in the public marketplace to those who simply **happened to be there**. Not those who he knew would be there, or those he prayed would be there or that God showed him would be there. Just those who happened to be there. Without any planning, preparation or selectivity, Paul simply spoke to those who, on the day he was there, also happened to be there.

For years we have missed this, we have not seen the power or potential of interacting with those who just happen to be there. We have been so busy looking for the open, the responsive and the ready that all too often we have ended up speaking to no one.

The *15 Revolution* is all about reaching out to those who just happened to be there. It is not selective, careful or focussed only on the apparently more open ones. The *15 Revolution* does not have the language or baggage of 'Lord, lead me to the right person'. As you can see from the various stories I have included, it's all about whoever just happens to be there. I see this same approach demonstrated in many other Bible stories but just consider Jesus himself. In the closing days of his life, Jesus stepped into the world of the Roman judicial and penal system.

When he arrived there he found numerous people already open to God: Pilate, who said 'I find no fault in him' and really wanted to free him. Pilate's wife, who'd had a disturbing dream about him. Simon from Cyrene who was press ganged into carrying his cross for him. The thief on the cross, who just happened to be on the same crucifixion schedule as Jesus and ended up in heaven. The centurion who oversaw the crucifixion who was wide open and declared, 'surely this man is the Son of God'. Joseph of Arimathea who gave his own tomb to Jesus.

All these people just happened to be there when Jesus arrived and those events unfolded. He didn't go looking for them, he just went with the invisible, effortless flow that governed his life. I believe there are people open to God among those who happen to be in your world too. You don't find them by going looking for them but by simply including all and loving all. They just happened to be there, now leave the rest to God – which is my next thought, so read on.

Starting the revolution

Debbie's Story

Well, today was the day I woke up and decided I would be proactive with this *15 Revolution* stuff. I would widen my view on the world and pay more attention to the people I moved among.

My first inconvenience didn't pay off. I made a special effort to leave home earlier and walk into the playground to drop the boys off at school, rather than dropping them off at the gate, watching them in and rushing off to work. I was hoping to have a revolution! So, I walked into the playground, scanning the parents, looking for someone in distress or collapsed on the floor or something! But everyone looked fine. They were all coping just fine without me. It did give me the opportunity to give the boys an extra hug, but that was it.

I walked back out of school, got in the car and drove home (still scanning pavements for people in distress!). After a day filled with 'scanning', my breakthrough moment came late on whilst at the gym. I had done my workout and was relaxing in the sauna when I found my opportunity to have a revolution moment.

There is a little lady at the gym whose job it is to clean the changing rooms. I have noticed her before sweeping, cleaning and hosing down the whole area. She goes around with her head down and I've never seen her smile - she normally looks fairly grumpy. Well, I could see her through the glass door shuffling around, sweeping and hoovering while people walked past her, splashing over her newly swept floor with their wet feet. That's when I had the idea to say thank you to her. So as I came out of the sauna room I was looking for her, but she disappeared into a cupboard room and I didn't want to stalk her! So I carried on getting sorted and getting my bags and then she came back round to where I was.I said 'You do a great job keeping all this clean and tidy'. She seemed surprised that someone had spoken to her and she smiled. 'It must be a pretty thankless task', I said 'you will have no sooner cleaned the floor than one of us comes out and gets water everywhere again!' She laughed and said 'yeah. I'm about ready to go home now'. So I said 'Well, just so you know, it is appreciated.' And that was it. It didn't take 15 minutes - but I hope it made her glad to have been noticed and thanked. I'll no doubt see her again and say hi and for me it's a start to my revolution (small r!).

Chapter 7

GOD IS SOVEREIGN

Paul's approach to those who just 'happened to be there' in Athens has another massive lesson to teach us about the *15 Revolution*. It is this: God is sovereign. And as such he sees, hears, and knows exactly who will just 'happen to be there'.

Paul had a very deep conviction that he was not God. Now that may sound an odd thing to say. But it is true. He was totally secure in the knowledge that God was sovereign, all-powerful and all-knowing, and that he would always operate in accordance with those attributes. He simply trusted his sovereign God whom he knew was entirely capable of organising for whoever was needed to be there at the same time as he was.

Throughout his life Paul did not try to predict or control outcomes or manipulate events. He simply trusted God's sovereign ability to make all things work together for good (Romans 8:28). Although Paul's going into the marketplace seems random and spontaneous, it was done from a fundamental confidence that God would take care of the 'who', 'where' and 'when', if he took care of explaining the 'what' and the 'why'.

What makes the *15 Revolution* so refreshing, effective and enjoyable is that it doesn't concern itself with whether it is reaching the right or wrong people; it just gets on with helping whoever happens to be there. I don't worry about whether you're the right person to have picked up this book, you just happened to have done so and I leave the rest to God. I don't concern myself with those who are not in the church service or at the conference, but only with those who happen to be there. I'm not concerned about all the people I should have met and missed because I wasn't there. I can only respond to those who happened to be there.

We were all once those who 'just happened to be there' before we were reached with the gospel. Looking back, we see that a certain moment became significant in our lives but, at the time, we just happened to be there. That is the sovereignty of God at work.

In our thirst for the significant and the spectacular, we charismatic Christians in particular have subscribed to a 'goose bump' Christianity. In so doing we have often despised the ordinariness of those who just happened to be there. We have tried to do the Holy Spirit's job by trying to be in all the right places at all the right times. We have sometimes tried to keep company with the who's who and get all the right people to attend our events. Well, the greatest Apostle who ever lived didn't bother with any of that; he just reached out to those who happened to be there and trusted the 'God who knows' for the rest. I've often thought that if God can get two of every kind of animal to make their way to Noah's Ark, then he can organise whoever he wants, to be wherever he wants, whenever he wants. If God can get non-migratory animals to make the journey to the ark and get animals that don't co-habit to live together, then he can arrange whoever happens to be there in our lives.

A game park ranger in Africa successfully spotted some wild elephants for us to observe. They are, of course, famed for their long memory and that got me thinking about which animal had the shortest memory. So I asked the ranger and without hesitation, he said 'a warthog'. Intrigued, I asked how he knew that. He replied 'when a lion chases a warthog, the warthog sets off running then suddenly stops and starts grazing, because it forgets why it is running. Then, when it sees the lion, it remembers why it was running and takes off again. Then it stops again and this goes on until either the lion gets fed-up, or the warthog is eaten'.

My point is this: if God can get two warthogs to find their way to Noah's Ark without forgetting where they are going, then getting the right people to the right place at the right time is relatively easy for him! So let's stop trying to control everything and just trust our sovereign God, the one who knows, and just be kind to whoever happens to be there.

A new friend just happened to be there

Esther's Story

On my way to university last week, I landed in the middle of hundreds of people in Belfast city centre standing together and listening to speeches about some local political issues. While trying to find a bus to bring me up to university a young Chinese girl caught my eye. She looked lost and confused and at that point I remembered the *15 Revolution*. I said 'hello' and asked if she was OK, to which she replied she didn't understand what was happening, and was also just trying to get a bus to university.

I told her I was going to university too and asked her if she wanted to come with me to find a bus. We eventually found a bus and, after paying, I went and sat beside her. She explained to me she had lived in China her whole life and had come to Northern Ireland to study the previous September. In a moment, I put myself into her shoes trying to understand how overwhelming it must have been to move such a distance from home with no family or friends. She explained to me she was finding it hard to meet friends as everyone she knew just loved to go out and party. At that point I invited her along to Rocknations, our youth group at church. I explained it would be a great way for her to meet new friends and build some great relationships. As we arrived at university we exchanged numbers and since then have kept in contact.

She is planning to come to youth on Friday night and church on Sunday morning. Because of the *15 Revolution*, not only did I get to help someone but I also met a really cool new friend.

Chapter 8

NOTHING JUST HAPPENS

Commenting on the location of people, Paul told the Athenians in Acts 17:26 that God *'determined the times set for them and the exact places where they should live. God did this so that men would seek him and perhaps reach out for him and find him, though he is not far from each one of us.'*

Paul is saying that God has placed all people within easy reach of himself. He consequently believed that God had placed enough of himself in everyone's world so that any who reached out to him would find him.

We have wrongly assumed that for people to be reached they must have a church or missionary or believer nearby. Of course, we want the possibility of that to increase but God is bigger than the church and is not confined to a gospel presentation to reach someone. Romans chapter 1 tells us that the Creation, all by itself, carries enough of God's invisible qualities and nature to reveal God to people. It means that no one will ever be able to say 'I had no idea God existed' and that everyone has the potential opportunity of reaching out to the creator God. Again, my point is that in his sovereignty, God has got it covered.

Returning to Athens, on the day that Paul was speaking in the marketplace, there just happened to be a group of philosophers present. These thinkers were members of the University of Athens or the Areopagus, a highly influential place. Intrigued by Paul's teaching they invited him to speak at the University. Paul went and spoke, and Luke sums up the response to him so realistically. He says, *'Some sneered' (v32), others said 'we want to hear you again on this subject' (v32) and a few 'became followers and believed' (v34).*

Doesn't that cover the typical range of response we all generally receive? If some sneered and others said 'maybe later' to the great Apostle Paul, then we shouldn't feel bad when it happens to us! Some won't accept the gospel, some want to hear more and a few are ready there and then to respond. That's the typical range of those who will be in your world this week.

Amongst those who believed Paul, was a man called Dionysius, a member of the Areopagus *(v34)*. This piece of information is highly significant because church history tells us that Dionysius, who came to Christ that day, went on to become the Bishop of Athens. He became the spiritual leader of the church in Athens and as a respected academic from the Areopagus, no doubt continued to have great influence on the developing minds of the next generation. Now that's a result! So let's just backtrack. Amongst those who 'happened to be there' in the marketplace were a group of philosophers from the university. They invited Paul to speak at their university and a man called Dionysius happened to be there, who happened to be ready to respond, and who happened to go on to become the Bishop of Athens. Now note that Paul did not go looking for Dionysius; he simply accepted that amongst whoever 'happened to be there' would be whoever God wanted there. Stop looking for Dionysius and just reach those who happen to be there. Dionysius wasn't even in the marketplace where the initial discussions took place, but those who could take Paul to him were. Sometimes, God will use whoever happens to be there to connect you with others who may not be there in person but are present in other people's lives.

Our constant challenge is to simply trust God for the fruit as we faithfully sow the seeds of being kind to people, sharing our lives with others and living out our faith.

The Bible is full of similar connections which are the result of people just faithfully doing what they knew they had to do with those who just 'happened to be there'. Take Ruth as another example. Before Ruth met Boaz and her fortunes changed, she only knew Naomi, who was a financially broke, three-times bereaved and desolate old woman with nothing tangible to offer young Ruth. But when Naomi encouraged her to leave and go back to her own country, Ruth stuck by Naomi. My point is that Ruth had no idea that Boaz was in her future. All she had was Naomi, a woman with no prospects, money, family or future to speak of. Ruth just loved her – the one who just 'happened to be there' - because she felt compassion and connection with her. If we do what is in front of us to do, who knows where it will lead? But if we bypass the ones who are here now in favour of the ones we wish were here now, we will never meet our 'Boaz'.

When you analyse it, underpinning Paul's understanding of God's sovereignty is a conviction that nothing 'just happens'. It was Paul who wrote, *'all things work together for good, for those that love God and are called according to his purpose' (Romans 8:28-31 NKJV).*

If all things work together for good, how many things are not working together for good? The answer is none! All things can be used by God. Even the things that are not sent by God can be used by God for the good of those who love him. This means nothing is ever wasted. Paul had a great many experiences, which were clearly not sent from God because there was evil intent behind them. But, in addition, he experienced all the things that 'just happen' because we live in a sin-poisoned world where much is beyond our immediate control. As we sometimes say, 'life happens!' It rains on the righteous and the unrighteous; the only difference is that the righteous try to find God in the rain, not just in the sunshine. Paul made sense of all this madness by seeing it in the light of his understanding of God's sovereignty. He wrote: *'We do not want you to be uninformed, brothers, about the hardships we suffered in the province of Asia. We were under great pressure, far beyond our ability to endure, so that we despaired even of life. Indeed, in our hearts we felt the sentence of death. But this happened that we might not rely on ourselves but on God, who raises the dead. He has delivered us from such a deadly peril, and he will deliver us. On him we have set our hope that he will continue to deliver us' (2 Corinthians 1:8-10).*

Paul realised that even bad things, frightening things, dangerous and difficult things all happen for a reason. He realised that they were designed to cause him not to rely on his own strength but on God's. Wow! What a precious thing to take from such an awful situation. Like many before him, Paul recognised that nothing 'just happens'; in everything there is something God can 'work together for good'.

Was Moses floated down the Nile in his baby basket for no reason? Was Joseph sold into slavery in Egypt for no reason? Was Esther taken into captivity in a foreign land for no reason? Was Daniel in captivity for no reason? Did Jonah just happen to board a boat going in the opposite direction to Nineveh, and there just happen to be a whale swimming around the boat when he got thrown overboard? 'No' is the answer to all these questions. In some cases, people made choices and exercised their free will, others were forced in a direction by people against their will. But in every case God used it! God remained in control, sovereignly overseeing the affairs of his people for his greater purpose. As Joseph said to his brothers who had sold him into slavery, *'Am I in the place of God? You intended to harm me, but God intended it for good to accomplish what is now being done, the saving of many lives' (Genesis 50:19).*

Nothing just happens, and those who join the *15 Revolution* enjoy the freedom of knowing that it doesn't matter whether we know where any single act of kindness will lead. What matters is being kind, even if it's just for 15 minutes a day.

Messed up - but in a good way

Gabrielle's Story

As I went into the supermarket last night for a quick shop I saw by the entrance a man selling The Big Issue magazine. I hadn't had my *15 Revolution* moment that day but thought to myself that I really just wanted to get home, so I would just give today a miss and give the man some money on my way out when I finished my shopping. I know it's selfish but it's what I thought.

Anyway, I went in, shopped, and went out. As I loaded my many bags into the boot of my car, I looked over at the man to whom I was going to give the pound coin from my shopping trolley and, as I looked at him, I thought 'has he had any food today? Would my pound even buy him a pack of gum?' I shut the boot of my car and said 'OK God, I'm sorry'.

I got over myself and my need to get home in a hurry, and went over and asked the man if I could buy him some groceries. He grinned and said 'that would be great'. I asked him what he liked and he was at a loss for words, as if no one had asked him that for a long time. He said, 'maybe some tins'. I said 'ok, what kind of tins?' He said 'some soup would be great'. I said is that all you want? Isn't there anything else I can get you? So he said milk and bread. I said ok, but is that all? He said, 'some tins' again.

As I started to walk away I think he started to get the point that I would get him whatever he wanted because he stopped me and said, could he have a pack of cigarettes? Now I know some would be disapproving but I instantly remembered how when I was lost, I used to LOVE a good cigarette. So I smiled and said 'sure, what kind?' He told me the kind he liked and off I went. I felt a bit cheeky but kept laughing as I went around the shop! I bought him everything I could think of, clothes, food, drinks, chocolate and to top it off I bought him two boxes of cigarettes and a multi pack of lighters to go with it.

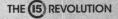

Controversial - yes, but I wanted his experience of meeting a Christian to be one of acceptance not one of, 'sorry sir you shouldn't smoke, don't you know that?' I put Abundant Life Church invitation cards in his huge bags of shopping, because I wanted to invite him to the Easter Sunday service. As I walked out of the supermarket, the man came out from behind the bin where he sat and he looked at his bags of shopping and said 'Oh my God'. He kept saying that over and over again, I couldn't even get a word in because when I handed him the bags he just turned and walked away saying 'Oh my God, oh my God, this is flipping wicked!'

So in the end I didn't get to invite him personally but I didn't care. He had food, clothes and cigs and it seemed to make his day! I hoped that, as he looked through his bags of goodies, he would find that invite card and would think of coming. But even if he didn't come, at least he knew for a moment that someone cared.

I went home to my house where my husband and my baby were. As I looked at my baby who belongs to us, I thought to myself that that man belonged to someone, yet he was alone and how blessed I was. It messed me up inside but in a good way. I will never look at a homeless person the same way again. That man was someone's son, brother or friend. If 15 minutes is all it took to make him feel important, like he mattered, then who am I to pass by that opportunity?

Chapter 9

MOBILISING THE MIDDLE

Every revolution evolves, and those who study their progress will often observe trends or problems that slow down, speed up or alter the path of the revolution.

A few months into the *15 Revolution*, I began to observe an interesting and significant phenomenon. I noticed that the people who got involved early on were mainly older, long standing Christians and church members. This was significant because, having led the same local church for many years, I have observed that these people tend to have the least un-churched friends. They are, therefore, least active in any kind of evangelism and least productive in terms of helping to grow the church numerically. This is not a complaint, nor is it exclusive to our church, it's simply an observation about their demographic and, I think, a widely accepted one. Anything that therefore mobilises this group of people outwards is of interest to me.

As the first wave of stories submitted by people about their *15 Revolution* experiences came in, I soon realised how well-suited the *15 Revolution* is to these often evangelistically dormant believers. You see, the qualities that best suit members of this revolution are compassion, inclusion of others, kindness, serving, generosity and empathy. And these mid-life believers have it in bucket loads! This revolution is simply asking these naturally compassionate, caring people to express that a little wider without calling it evangelism.

I remain convinced that if I had initially presented the *15 Revolution* idea as an evangelistic initiative, this group would have largely avoided it. That's the strength of the *15 Revolution*! It mobilises the middle ground, the believers who have years of experience, lots to offer, but which is in many instances locked up in pastoral roles within the church rather than being expressed in the community.

For the first time in years, I began receiving letters and stories from many of these long-standing church members. Many had come to life and, for the first time in a long time, had experienced the joy of connecting with un-churched people through natural benevolence and acts of kindness.

Helping strangers

A second observation I made as the *15 Revolution* gathered momentum, was that every story was almost exclusively about helping strangers. This, I realised, is potentially huge because I have always believed that the greatest harvest for our churches is among the strangers in our community, not among people we know.

Our challenge, in an un-churched nation like England, is to understand how we can best approach these often anti-church strangers. Well, here was an answer! Goodness and kindness are bridges over which anything can travel. And older believers usually have plenty of kindness and love to give away.

It is a fact of life that we all default to keeping company with those we find it easiest to be with. We all prefer the comfort and familiarity of those who know and love us over those who don't. My hairdresser story after Chapter 1 re-enforced that principle to me, because I didn't want to spend an hour with a stranger. I wanted the comfort of my usual, but totally unresponsive, hairdresser. For three years, I completely ignored everyone else at my hairdressers because I pre-set my mind about my usual routine, all the while praying that God would use me to reach people! It's as if sometimes God is saying I want to use you, but you've got stuck in Comfortville!

Jesus told his team, don't say *'Four months more and then the harvest? I tell you, open your eyes and look at the fields! They are ripe for harvest' (John 4:35).*

Clearly harvest often depends on where you're looking. So many of us are stuck in a comfortable but tiny circle of love, and to widen that circle to strangers feels particularly awkward because we think that involves evangelism. But our connection to new people shouldn't be trying to convert them; it should, first and foremost, be to befriend them.

The language of love, grace, kindness and inclusion is universal and will pave the way for the gospel and all the connections our sovereign God knows lie ahead in the life of the people concerned.

So, get out of your comfort zone and join the Revolution!

Meeting the neighbours

Katrina's Story

In my life, it's pretty normal to step in and help people I see along my travels whether they be a homeless person, an old lady who needs her shopping carrying or a lost little child. It's a nice feeling to be the 'hero' to people you are likely never to meet again, but for me the *15 Revolution* has hit a bit closer to home... like on my street with neighbours who aren't in need, who are very capable of carrying their own shopping and with whom there is little opportunity to interact.

There is one couple three doors down from me who moved in over 8 months ago and who I have never even said hello to - just because there just never seemed a good reason or opportunity.

So, the *15 Revolution* teaching comes along and I notice that she has had a baby (I didn't even know she was pregnant - see what I mean!!) Normally, I would have just got on with my busy life and thought 'good for them' but this time I decided to drive to a store, buy a card and some flowers and knock on the door. I said 'Hi', gave her the flowers and card, had a lovely 15 min chat with her and was able to just give this first time mum some friendly encouragement about the joys of parenting.

That was it. No hero time, no walking away feeling like I've changed someone's life or that it was a 'divine appointment'. But I do feel like I can at least say I know my neighbour's name, and that can only be a good thing! And just look at this *15 Revolution* scripture I read today:

'Those of us who are strong and able in the faith need to lend a hand to those who falter and not just do what is ***most convenient for us****. Strength is for service, not status. Each of us needs* ***to look after the good of the people around us asking ourselves: "How can I help?"*** *(Romans 15:1 - The Message)*

Chapter 10

REVOLUTIONARY STORIES

Since I first taught the principles outlined in this short book, stories have flooded in as people have taken up my challenge to 'join the revolution'. Many were initially from the congregations of my home church in Bradford, Leeds and Belfast. But, increasingly, they are coming from around the world as the revolution spreads.

This final chapter is dedicated to some of those stories, all of which were posted on the *15 Revolution* website by the writers. They are reproduced here, with their permission, and in their own words, but all names have been omitted or changed to protect people's privacy. But one thing's for sure; all these contributors are 15 Revolutionaries! And I salute them for sharing their experiences with us. I pray they will inspire you to join the revolution.

Enjoy!

A helping hand

Lucy's Story

I was waiting at the self-serve checkout, with about three or four in the queue, when I looked up and saw an old very scruffy-looking man standing at one of the self-serve tills looking very confused. I waited a few minutes to see if the attendant would help him, but she did nothing. She didn't even ask if he was ok!

At this point a man got fed up of waiting and pushed himself in front of him, put his own shopping through and walked off while this poor man was just stood there. It made me really mad! So, as another person was about to do the same thing, I shoved myself in front of them and stood next to this man at the till point. I put my shopping down and asked him if he was ok. He said he didn't know how to use the self-serve tills, so I offered to put his shopping through and show him. So I went through his shopping, bagged it for him, and he gave me the money. When I gave him his change, he took my hands. He smelt of alcohol and my heart sank for him. He held my hands so tight, thanked me, and told me he didn't finish school so couldn't read or write and that he appreciated me taking the time to help him. I helped him with his bags and off he went. It really shocked me that people could be so ignorant and how they could just ignore someone who so obviously needed help. That's why this 15 Revolution is so amazing. If we all just do our bit, maybe we can change things and make this non-caring attitude a thing of the past!

The flat tyre

Andy's Story

Whilst driving home through the rush hour traffic, I passed a cyclist who was pushing his bike along the pavement because the back tyre was flat. It was very difficult and not safe to pull over immediately, so I drove to the next roundabout, drove back up the road past the cyclist to a place where I could turn back around safely, and drove back down the road until I came alongside him. As I stopped, I asked him if he wanted to put the bike in the back of my truck and I would give him a lift home. He was so grateful, he told me he cycles to work and back everyday and was dressed up in all the cycling gear - helmet, shoes, lycra, the lot! I couldn't help but think how many people had driven past him without giving him or his situation a second thought. I asked him his name and what he did for a living and Jason told me a little about himself as we drove along. He asked me a couple of times if I was going out of my way to take him home, or did I really drive that way home myself, to which I said; I was going that way anyway'. I dropped him off at the end of his street and drove off.

Out of the comfort zone

Carl's Story

Whilst shopping today in Belfast, I walked past a gentleman who looked like he'd seen better days. He looked like a bit of an outcast really. My heart went out to him and I thought - maybe I should ask him if he wants to have lunch. I would never normally do this, as it's a bit weird when a complete stranger walks up to you and asks you if you want to hang out! But I really felt like this guy needed someone to talk to. So, I thought I'd step out of my comfort zone and do it anyway!

I tapped him on the shoulder, he turned around and I introduced myself to him. He said his name was Martin. I said, 'Are you up for having a bite to eat?' He said, 'Oh yes that would be brilliant.' We walked into the coffee shop across the way and sat down after ordering some coffee and food. I talked to him about the troubles in Belfast - he knew a lot about the history of Ireland. I asked him about his life - he seemed a lonely person. He couldn't speak very well and had a strong stutter - so it was hard to understand him at times. He asked me about my life as well and I shared my faith with him. He told me he was a Christian, which was brilliant.

This experience for me was out of my comfort zone completely. It could have backfired, but it just shows you how open people can be to some company. There are a lot of lonely people out there.

The faces behind the windows

Jane's Story

For 60 of my mum's 81 years, she has been institutionalised. From the age of 21, she was admitted to a mental hospital. Today she is happy and content in a small family-run residential home in the village where she was born. I have visited her twice a week for the four years she has been in this home. On every visit mum's first words were 'Are we going out for a cig?' (I don't smoke - so it was the 'royal we').

Whatever the weather, rain, hail, snow or sun, we were outside, maybe sitting comfortably in the sun, or huddled under an umbrella whilst mum devoured as many 'cigs' as she possibly could. This was her only pleasure, and bearing in mind the life she had had, I felt why not? She had very little quality of life. The times we spent outdoors gave me a chance to peep through the windows and glimpse the other residents inside. The faces staring back looked sad, lonely and empty. I would tap on the window and wave. Sometimes I got a response but mainly nothing. 'Waiting for God' comes to mind. Mum said, 'nobody in that room gets a visitor'. Last November, mum was very ill. She had a few mini strokes throughout the year. I would get a call from the home - could I please go urgently because the ambulance was due to arrive. I would dash over, expecting the worst and, yes, the ambulance was in the grounds with mum inside. I'd step inside the ambulance where mum was laid out on the bed. The minute she saw me she shot up and said 'Are we going out for a cig?' She refused to go to hospital and became very agitated. This happened again and again.

But, November was different. She was not responding to anything or anyone, so hospital it was. I was mentally planning her funeral, she was so ill. Two days in hospital and not getting any better. On the third day I entered the ward to be greeted with 'Oh good, you're here, I can go out for a cig'. Mum was sitting up in bed as large as life. On her return to her 'home' it was decided that instead of sitting in her room alone, mum would have to sit with the other residents in the 'lounge'. She did need assistance with walking etc so it was easier for the staff to keep their eye on her. So, when I visited, I would be getting the chance to meet the 'faces' behind the windows:

There's Faye, who at 89, tells me she has had such a busy day in the office and is ready for a gin and lime. In her mind, she still 'works' for BP! There's Henry, he has just turned 83. A real ladies man, who tells me that all the ladies in there are queuing up to get into his bed? Well, he can dream, bless him. He loves to dance with me and tell me he wants to stay in my arms forever. He gives me the biggest longest hug when it's time for me to leave. He relates his time in the war, and his school days and trillions of his memories come flooding out, as do his tears. There's Chrissie, who is always dressed for 'going out to bingo' with a friend who doesn't exist and, for the most part, is in her own little world. She shied away from me when I first tried to give her a hug, so I didn't approach her on my next visit and just knelt down in front of her to say goodbye. She put her arms out and said 'don't forget me'. There's mum who - wait for it - hasn't mentioned a 'cig' once since coming home. There was also Ron and Barbara. Sadly they passed away within a couple of weeks of each other, but we had lots of fun and chat. We sing lots of old songs like 'Daisy, daisy give me your answer do', and 'We'll meet again'. Amazingly, I seem to know the words - that must be God, as I can't possibly be that old! Then there are the three ladies who never seem to be awake. But one thing is certain, they all love chocolate...

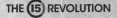

...This brings me to my next related 15 Revolution: I was at our local garage paying for petrol and nine bars of chocolate for my visit. The lady looked at me and said 'Are we baking a chocolate cake today love?' I old her who the chocolate was for and she said 'That's a lovely thought'. Suddenly she broke down in tears and revealed that she had found it necessary to put her mum in a home five years ago and couldn't get over the guilt she felt. By this time, there was quite a queue forming behind me. One of her colleagues came to the rescue and I took Mary (her name badge told me that) to one side. She was so upset by the fact that she couldn't look after her mum and sobbed and sobbed. I put my arm around her and tried to reassure her she had done the right thing. She dried her eyes and smiled at me and thanked me for listening. I haven't seen her since. But maybe she is doing her own 15 Revolution at her mum's care home!

A tow

Dan's Story

Whilst driving down the bypass on my way home one night, I noticed a car on the other side of the road that was on the grass verge, engine cover up and hazard lights on. Obviously it had broken down. I drove to the next roundabout, turned round and drove back to where the car was. I pulled up in front of the car, got out and asked if I could help. The young lad, whose car it was, told me he had run out of petrol and I offered to tow him to a garage. My truck does not have a proper towing 'eye' so I improvised and looped the towrope around the chassis of my truck and steadily towed him to the nearest garage so he could fill up. When we got there, I hung around to make sure his car would start when he'd filled up, and once the car was running again I said goodbye and went to leave. He offered me money for helping him, which I politely refused, and went home.

Sowing and reaping the revolution

John's Story

I think the 15 Revolution is a two way thing. If you put an 'Inconvenience Me' sign on the door of your heart, then I believe other people, total strangers, will go out of their way to help you too.

I have an extraordinary story of how the Oscar winning writer of Slumdog Millionaire, Simon Beaufoy, inconvenienced himself for me! On Tuesday night, Simon was giving an interview as part of the Bradford Film Festival with a Q&A session afterwards.

I bought my ticket and went along armed with my question and hoping I would get the chance to ask it. I did. I said 'I'm a graduate of the Northern Film School who has a script that I've written being looked at by Universal Studios in Hollywood. What advice would you give to someone in my position seeking to get their first feature film script made?' He said 'get representation, an Agent.' I went on to explain that all the agents I'd contacted had replied saying 'under the current economic climate we are not extending our client list.' He then said, 'I'd like to talk more with you, come and see me afterwards.'

After the Q&A, there were lots of people hanging around wanting his autograph and to hold the Oscar that he had brought along. When things had quietened down I approached him. He asked how I had managed to get my script into the hands of a Hollywood executive. I told him a friend of mine was in LA last year for a round of meetings with Universal, they didn't take his film but they asked if he had something with a budget of $40-50 million dollars, so my friend pitched my story, (which, if you're curious, is about Leonardo da Vinci during the time he lived in Milan and painted 'The Last Supper'). Universal took the script in January and I'm waiting to hear back. I told Simon about the various production companies in the UK who had looked at it and the favourable comments that I had back, but that most had baulked at the budget, which is way above most British film companies, and the problems I was having trying to get an agent. Simon thought for a minute and said, 'I'm going to help you. Have you got a business card?' I gave him my business card and he said he's going to have a think about who best to pass my details on to, but not to worry, he will speak to someone about my script. I was delighted and thanked him and went on my way.

I never expected such a magnanimous gesture from such an obviously busy man, who must be inundated with requests. But he was warm, friendly and, being a Yorkshire lad, very down to earth. All I can do now is trust him and wait to hear from someone who he passes my details onto. Phew! I'm still buzzing!

The power of a smile

Sue's Story

Had a great *15 Revolution* this weekend whilst over in Belfast with a team of Leadership Academy students. We'd gone to help with a Mothers' Day outreach event. After blessing mothers with chocolate, cakes and hugs for Mothers' Day with the church team, which was fantabulous, I took time out to meet up with my brother. As I stood waiting for him, I noticed a homeless guy sitting by the side of the street.

My initial thought was 'I don't have any money to give, I can't really do anything for him'. But then I thought 'well I do have a smile, and I have words'. So I went over to chat to him. I said, 'Hello, how are you doing, I'm Sue, what's your name?' His response to me was a very puzzled look! Then I realised that he was foreign and didn't really speak English. I thought 'Oh rubbish! What am I going to do now? I can't just walk away!' So I pointed to myself and repeated 'Sue' and pointed to him and he said 'Ostika'. So we exchanged names, I think! Again, a silence. There wasn't really anything else I could do. So I just sat down on the pavement beside him. We sat together for a while people watching until my brother came and I said good bye. Me and my brother went to a cafe for a drink so I thought 'I'll get Ostika a cup of tea'. I took it back and gave it to him and in return he gave me the biggest smile I think I'd seen all day! He took the cup of tea, put it on the floor then took a hold of my hand, looked right at me and said a meaningful 'God Bless'! Wow!! How amazing, Ostika hardly knew any English, but he knew the words God bless! Ostika's words really impacted me, I think even more than my cup of tea impacted him!

A cup of tea

Sharon's Story

I was walking to meet my friend in the rain and I saw a homeless person sleeping in a doorway. I took this opportunity to buy the guy a cup of tea.

Taking time to notice people

Ruth's Story

I'm a music teacher at a very challenging inner city school. It's a boys' school and the vast majority of the students are of Pakistani-Muslim heritage. It's a school where emphasis is often placed on students' poor behaviour and under-achievement. Because of these problems, those boys who deserve to be noticed seem to get lost, because so much attention is given to those who cause or have problems.

A few weeks ago I was going through my teacher's planner in order to inform the writing of student reports. This is not a job I usually enjoy and can often be a tedious task. I noticed the marks and codes I had put in my planner for one boy in particular, who had been doing consistently well in both written and practical tasks. The boy is 11 years old and a quiet and well behaved lad who I had hardly noticed before, and didn't know much about. The next time I had his class, I took a few moments at the end of the lesson to chat with him. I told him how pleased I was with him and he was visibly standing taller at the end of our chat. He began attending choir rehearsals and I noticed he has an excellent singing voice and a natural talent for music.

Since then, I have encouraged him more and he has shown a real gift for music. I am now giving up time during one of my non-teaching periods to teach him one-to-one in piano and singing. I telephoned home to talk to his parents about how well he has been doing, only to discover that both his parents had died when he was quite young and that he lived with an Aunt and Uncle. I am really glad that I took the time to get to know this boy who now has the opportunity to foster his musical talent. The other day he said to me 'Thank you so much for thinking of me Miss'. It's amazing what God can do when you take the time to notice people!

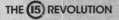

God's perfect timing

Sheryl's Story

I had been on car park duty at church all day so I was very tired from a busy day. It had also been raining all day, so I was soaked. I decided that once we had finished on car park at 8:30pm I was going to go straight home and not hang about. Once we'd cleared up, I saw a friend, so I stayed to chat and didn't end up leaving until 10pm - much later than I had intended! On my journey home, there had been a really bad car crash. There were about four or five cars involved. In the middle of the road was a woman alone in her smashed - up car.

I had a split second decision to make - do I help her or do I leave her? In my mind, I was weighing up the dangers and I could hear my mum's voice in the back of my mind saying 'No it's too dangerous and you are alone at night'. But this woman needed help and there were loads of people stood just watching but not helping. As I pulled over, I knew that if I was helping someone in need, which is what Jesus would have done,

God would protect me and keep me safe. So I ran over to the wrecked car and pulled open the door with all the strength I had. When I'd dragged the door open, I asked the lady if she was ok and if she hurt anywhere. Once I knew she was fine to walk, I assisted her out of the car and sat her on the side walk. I stayed with her until the ambulance and her family arrived. Once I'd learned she was ok, I headed home. So, if I'd have just gone home when I originally wanted, I would have totally missed out on a window of opportunity that God placed before me. But instead, I was able to show God's love by being there. Remember, no matter how much you may want to do something or what your plans are, it's not about us, it's about others.

The tangible love of God

Alex's Story

Last night I had a 15 Revolution moment! My electric went at home, so I went into town to get a McDonald's as I had no way of cooking any food. When I had bought my meal, I went to sit down and a teenage girl said, 'You won't be able to eat your food with that smell in here' and glanced over at a sad-looking lady in the corner. Hearing that prompted me to grab the seat nearest to the lady. I knew that's what Jesus would have done and he wanted me to love on her! The lady eventually asked me if had 20p, so I gave her a bit more. I looked at her table and said, 'Is that all you've had to eat?' She told me it was and so I told her I'd buy her a meal. But all she wanted was an ice-cream, so I bought her one and listened as she talked about various problems she was having. She just wanted someone to take an interest in her and I was more than happy to do so!

As I went to leave, I told her that it was lovely to meet her and told her to take care. As I glanced back, she had the biggest smile on her face! I just hope that when she went to bed that night, she didn't remember the negative comment that girl made, but that she remembered being loved on by a girl she may never meet again. I hope she discovered the tangible love of God!

Taking an interest

Marissa's Story

I live on the top floor of a house that has been converted into two apartments. Beneath us we have a lovely elderly gentleman. We are constantly passing each other as we come and go through the week. He lives simply and on his own. I recently had some time off from work and he invited me over for a cup of tea. I was a bit inconvenienced as I had planned to do other things. But I decided to have a cup of tea with my elderly neighbour.

Conversation wasn't easy but he was delighted to have someone show some interest in his world, he even showed me the uniform he wears, as he belongs to two male voice choirs and one mixed choir. At most, it took twenty minutes of my time, sealed with an awkward kiss on the cheek, and a comment from him saying he would like to come with me sometime to 'that Abundant Life Church!'

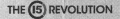

The beautiful Grandma

Joanne's Story

I was at the supermarket checkout and an old lady (she must have been at least 90) was loading her weekly shop onto the conveyor belt. I felt a little sad that she was alone at her age doing her own shopping with no help etc. It just seemed wrong!

She said to the guy on checkout 'Can you let me know how much my bill is before you put this book through so that I know I have enough'. Her shopping came to £12 and her book was an extra £3.50 so she told him she didn't want it. Anyway, I said to the guy, 'Can you please let me pay for all her shopping and the book'. He said to the lovely old lady 'this young lady wants to pay for it for you' (she thought he meant the book only) and she was really overwhelmed. I paid and then she asked the guy how much the rest of the shopping was and, when she realised I had paid for it all, she just broke down. I said to her, 'If I had a beautiful grandma like you I would treat her, but as I don't, I want to do the same for you'. She remarked 'God will so bless you for this, thank you so much' and she couldn't stop looking back and thanking me as she walked out of the store.

A few buns

Louise's Story

There is a vulnerable mum who lives across my street and I thought she and her children would be blessed if I made some buns. I did so, however, they sunk a little in the middle. This, plus a family member who was negative to the idea, meant that my confidence went and I did not give the buns away. I was rather disappointed and so asked God to let me have another go. I made more buns and this time the buns looked better. I had made up my mind not to be dissuaded by anyone. The mum was delighted and so grateful I was able to do a little something for her. I want to note the importance of not being dissuaded and say that if you have an idea to help someone, just to go for it. How exciting to think of all the people in our city being blessed each day because of the 15 Revolution and how great it is to be a part of it!

A cup of coffee

Tom's Story

I came across a homeless guy who was begging on the pavement outside a shop. Rather than just give him money and walk off, I asked him if he wanted anything to eat or drink. He told me he had eaten and would like a cup of coffee, so I asked him where there was a shop I could get one from. He told me there was a cafe across town, gave me directions, and I went to find it. I found a cafe, bought a coffee, and walked back to where he was. Upon handing him the coffee, he looked at the cup and told me that I'd gone to the wrong cafe because the one he told me to go to sold better coffee in bigger cups! Anyway, he took the coffee from me. I asked him his name, which he told me. We chatted briefly and I told him it had been nice meeting him and then left.

Simple kindness

Beccy's Story

On Friday evening I found a homeless guy looking through the bins at Foster Square and asked him if he was hungry. I took him to McDonalds where he got a big feed. I sat with him and he had a meal, dessert and a coffee to take away with him. At the end he said to me 'Why on earth would you be nice to me?' I said, 'Because I go to the Abundant Life Church, and we just love to be kind to people to give them a glimpse of how much God loves them by a simple act of kindness.' He then began to get teary, and said no one had ever been as kind to him. Amazing!

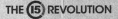

EPILOGUE

Ok, that's it. That's the book. I'm not going to make it longer than it needs to be. Short is good! These thoughts have been more than enough to inspire and mobilise our church and many others around the world into the *15 Revolution*, and hopefully they are enough to inspire you.

I'm not trying to offer some complex new theology or evangelistic concept. This is more about mobilisation than theology. We are all by nature, and many of us by nurture, selfish. So without a revolution of some kind, that innate selfishness always wins in the end.

We do not default to helping others; we have to constantly choose it. Helping others can be a huge nameless, faceless concept. It can even be our theology. But without a revolution against our default mode it can never be our practice.

The *15 Revolution* is my attempt to bring helping others right down to our 'now'! It is immediate and instantly accessible to all, old and young alike.

It may be no revolution to you; maybe helping others is natural to you. If so, I promise you that you're the exception not the norm. If you find this easy, I salute you and ask you to help the rest of us to join the revolution.

Finally, to all who get involved in this revolution, I invite you to visit the **www.15revolution.com** website and tell others your story. The more stories, the greater the understanding and inspiration we will all gain from each other.

"I was hungry and you fed me, I was thirsty and you gave me something to drink, I was a stranger and you invited me in. I needed clothes and you clothed me, I was sick and you looked after me, I was in prison and you came to visit me." Then the righteous will answer him, "Lord when did we all do this?"' (Matthew 25:35-40).

Then the King may well answer, 'you did it 15 minutes at a time and that's why you never realised the difference you were making!'

May this be the start of your *15 Revolution*.

Let the revolution begin.

Long live the revolution!

To read more
15 Revolution stories or
to send your own
go to:

WWW.15REVOLUTION.COM

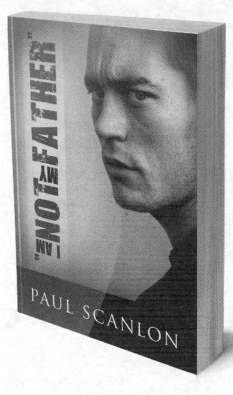

Also available by Paul Scanlon:

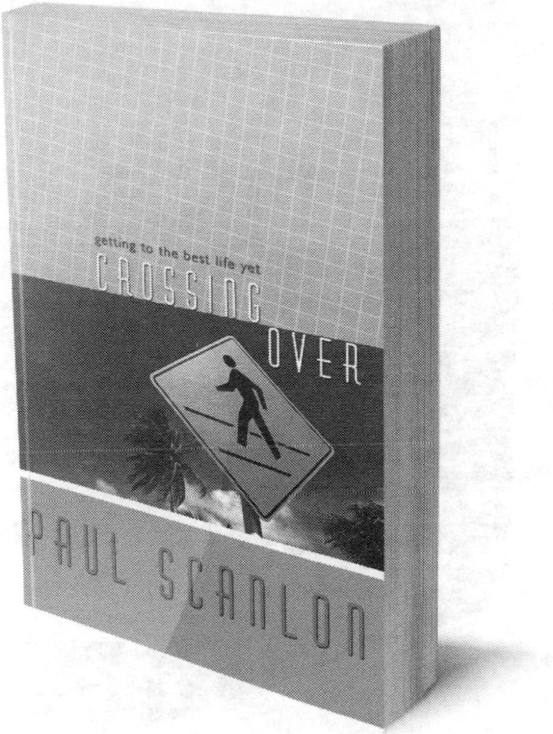

Crossing Over

This book is the essential guide for your journey from complacency to passion. It will challenge your sense of comfort, urge you to step out into unknown territory and to help you get to your best life yet. The Church of tomorrow is wrapped up in the decisions you make today.

www.alm.org.uk/shop

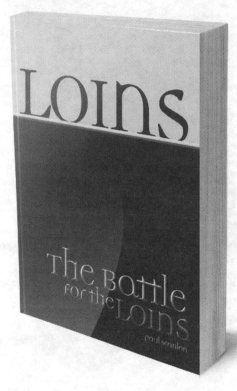

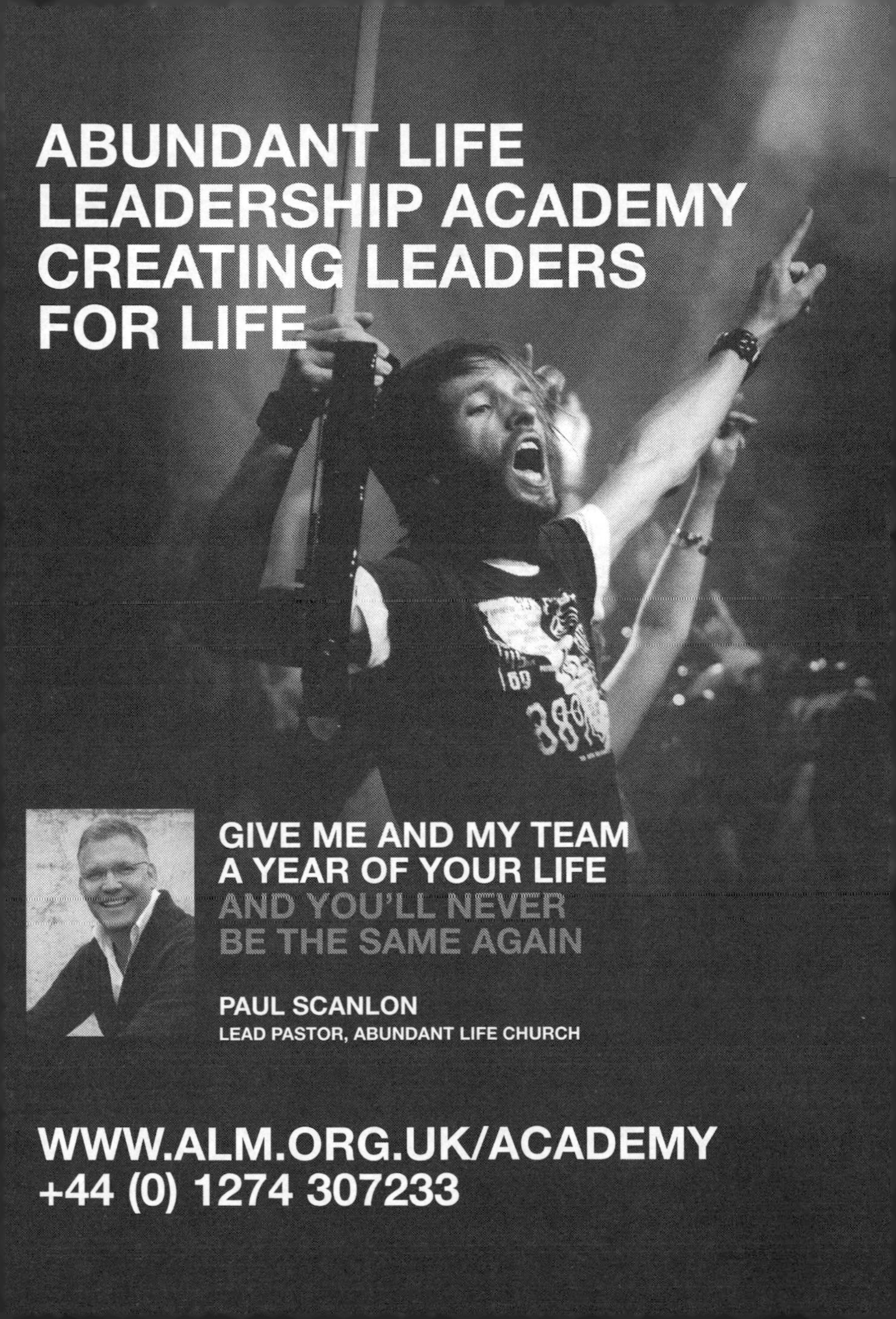
ABUNDANT LIFE
LEADERSHIP ACADEMY
CREATING LEADERS
FOR LIFE
GIVE ME AND MY TEAM
A YEAR OF YOUR LIFE
AND YOU'LL NEVER
BE THE SAME AGAIN
PAUL SCANLON
LEAD PASTOR, ABUNDANT LIFE CHURCH
WWW.ALM.ORG.UK/ACADEMY
+44 (0) 1274 307233